Spring Festivals Around the World

Elaine A. Kule

Rigby
A Harcourt Achieve Imprint

www.Rigby.com
1-800-531-5015

CHAPTER 1

Spring: An Introduction

The weather turns warmer, there are more hours of daylight, and suddenly you notice that it is spring. Have you ever wondered why the seasons change?

The changes in seasons come from Earth's yearly trip around the sun. As our planet travels along its **orbit**, the North Pole is tilted toward the sun for part of the year. During this time, the sun's rays hit the northern half of the world more directly. The **Northern Hemisphere** then experiences summer.

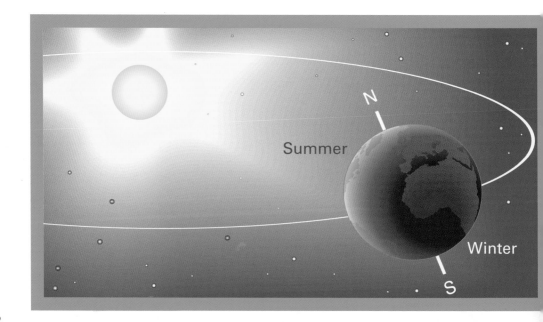

While the North Pole is tilted toward the sun, the South Pole is tilted away from it. The sun's rays hit the southern half of Earth less directly, so it is winter there. When it is summer in the United States, for example, it is winter in Australia.

While we enjoy summer in the United States, Australia is in the middle of their winter.

In between winter and summer is the **vernal equinox**, when day and night are each twelve hours long. It is the first day of spring in places north of the **equator**. Spring brings warmer weather and longer days. South of the equator, it is the first day of autumn, when the weather turns colder and the days get shorter.

Spring's warmer temperatures and added hours of daylight help flowers bloom and crops grow. Since ancient times, people have understood the importance of spring and celebrated its yearly arrival.

In the Northern Hemisphere, the first day of spring falls on March 20 or March 21. The United States is in the Northern Hemisphere.

In ancient times family and friends came together, often outdoors, to share large meals. Music, singing, and dancing were also a part of these events, or festivals.

Spring festivals are still celebrated in countries throughout the world. They may last for one day or for several weeks.

Come along and learn about some of these festivals. Our first stop is China.

CHAPTER 2

China: Spring Festival

In ancient China, most people were farmers. Chinese scientists spent centuries developing a calendar that showed people when to plant crops for a successful **harvest**.

Since spring was so important to the people in China, it was decided that each year of the Chinese calendar would begin when spring came. The Chinese New Year became known as the Spring Festival.

Beijing

CHINA

N
E
W
S

China has the largest population of any country in the world. Its capital city is Beijing.

The Spring Festival (which lasts for 15 days) is still the most important celebration among the Chinese people. The idea of a new beginning for a new year is a large part of the celebration.

Homes and shops are cleaned, and new clothes are worn. Flowers, the symbols of spring, are bought to decorate homes, shops, and offices, and to give as gifts. Some Chinese people think that the larger a flower blooms, the richer its owner will be in the new year.

Buying flowers is a tradition of the Spring Festival, also known as the Chinese New Year.

7

People eat special foods during the Spring Festival that represent wishes for the new year.

On the night before the first day of the celebration, many families gather to enjoy a big meal. Some foods **symbolize** wishes for a happy future. Round dumplings, for example, symbolize coins and the hope that money will come to those who eat the dumplings. Long noodles are thought to symbolize a long life.

After dinner most people watch holiday programs on television. They try to stay up all night to welcome in the new year.

Chinese people also celebrate the Chinese New Year with parades through the main streets of their communities. Dancers wear colorful lion and dragon costumes. In the Chinese culture, lions and dragons represent strength and good luck. Acrobats, stilt-walkers, and musicians playing drums, cymbals, and gongs are in the parade, too. It's all very loud and festive.

No Chinese New Year or Spring Festival parade would be complete without dragon dancers. They hold up the dragon with poles.

9

CHAPTER 3
India: Festival of Colors

Leaving China, we travel to India, a country in southern Asia. Many Indian people are farmers, and because they plant crops in the spring, the season is very important to them as well. Every March the country holds an ancient celebration to honor spring called the Festival of Colors.

New Delhi

INDIA

India has the second largest population of any country in the world. Its capital city is New Delhi.

Laddu is made with nuts, butter, sugar, raisins, and more.

During this time, large meals are shared with family and friends. Holiday treats include *laddu*, a fried and sweetened ball of dough, and *mathri*, a salty, fried snack usually eaten along with a pickle. Later, people gather around outdoor fires and wish for a good harvest.

During the holiday, shops, offices, and schools are closed. Many people wear white clothing. They continue the ancient tradition of spraying each other with *gulal*, which is made from flowers and plants that are dried and ground into powders. The different colored powders are packed in small plastic bags.

The Festival of Colors celebrates the beautiful shades of spring.

People also paint their faces and throw water balloons filled with *gulal* at anyone passing by. By the end of the day, many people's clothes are no longer white!

People dance and enjoy throwing water balloons filled with dyed water at each other on this day.

CHAPTER 4

United States: Earth Day

The term "spring cleaning" came into use in the middle 1800s, but people started cleaning for the season long before then. The warmer weather encouraged them to clean up the dirt and clear away the clutter that gathered during the winter.

Spring's arrival inspired the cleaning of homes, shops, and offices. But it would take many years for "spring cleaning" to include tidying Earth, too!

On April 22, 1970, the first Earth Day was celebrated in the United States. People were afraid that the planet's air and water supply was being destroyed, and they wanted to do something to change it. They planned a large celebration that took place across the country and about 20 million people took part in the event. Speakers talked about the dangers of **pollution** and wasting Earth's natural resources. They encouraged people to take action to help Earth.

Planting a garden is one way to improve Earth.

15

That first Earth Day had a powerful effect on the nation. Even the United States Congress took action and created the Environmental Protection Agency (EPA). The EPA created pollution standards that businesses must follow. The EPA has strict rules for landfills to make sure that trash doesn't pollute the land or the water.

Ways to Celebrate Earth Day

1. Clean your room!
2. Ask an adult to help you plant flowers in your yard or neighborhood.
3. Don't waste paper or electricity.
4. Recycle cans and plastic bags.
5. Read books to find out more about saving our planet.
6. Tell other people what you've learned about Earth Day.

Earth Day later included the idea of cleaning up Earth by picking up litter found in streets, parks, and beaches. People also are learning to cut down on garbage by recycling items such as paper and plastic bags. Earth Day is celebrated on the first day of spring by some people and on April 22 by others. Many countries around the world also take part in Earth Day celebrations.

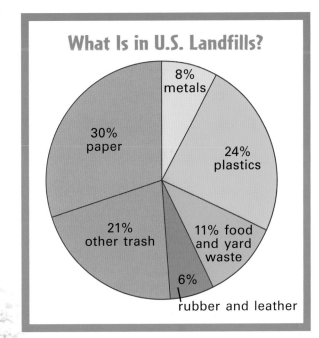

What Is in U.S. Landfills?

8% metals
30% paper
24% plastics
21% other trash
11% food and yard waste
6% rubber and leather

Landfill companies must follow the rules made by the EPA. These rules decide things such as how big a landfill can be and how far it must be from sources of drinking water.

CHAPTER 5

Japan: Cherry Blossom Festival

In Japan people know that spring has arrived when light pink cherry blossoms appear on trees. Because there are different climates throughout the country, the trees bloom at different times, from early March to early April. For this reason, the nation's Cherry Blossom Festival is a month of celebrations instead of a single day's event.

Since cherry blossoms last only one week, it's important to know when they'll bloom. The blossom forecast is announced every year by Japan's weather department.

JAPAN

Tokyo

In Tokyo, Japan's capital, cherry blossoms appear at the end of March.

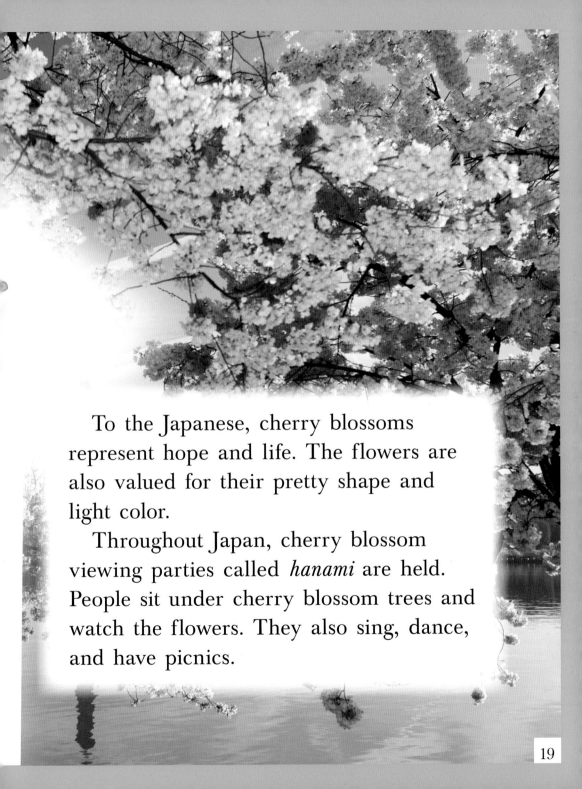

To the Japanese, cherry blossoms represent hope and life. The flowers are also valued for their pretty shape and light color.

Throughout Japan, cherry blossom viewing parties called *hanami* are held. People sit under cherry blossom trees and watch the flowers. They also sing, dance, and have picnics.

In a large city like Tokyo, the best viewing spots go quickly. Many people arrive early with blankets and sit in their places all day and evening. After the sun goes down, they hang paper lanterns in the trees.

The famous Cherry Dance, or *Miyako Odori*, has become part of the festival in Japan's larger cities. Women dancers wear beautiful silk robes, or kimonos, during their graceful performances.

This woman is performing the Cherry Dance. It has nine scenes.

In March 1912, Yukio Ozaki, the mayor of Tokyo, brought 3,000 cherry trees to Washington, D.C. The gift was in honor of the growing friendship between the United States and Japan. Since 1935, a yearly Cherry Blossom Festival has been held in Washington, D.C. to remember the event.

Hundreds of thousands of visitors come to Washington, D.C. to see the trees during the Cherry Blossom Festival.

In 1994 the Washington, D.C. Cherry Blossom Festival was made two weeks long. People spend the two weeks enjoying art displays, classes about cherry blossoms, and kimono fashion shows. On the festival's last day, the National Cherry Blossom Parade is held, followed by a street fair celebrating Japanese culture.

More than 700,000 people visit Washington, D.C. each year. While welcoming spring, they also see the lovely gifts Japan gave the U.S. almost one hundred years ago.

Washington, D.C. isn't the only city to hold a festival. Other cities, such as Chicago and San Francisco, also have Cherry Blossom Festivals.

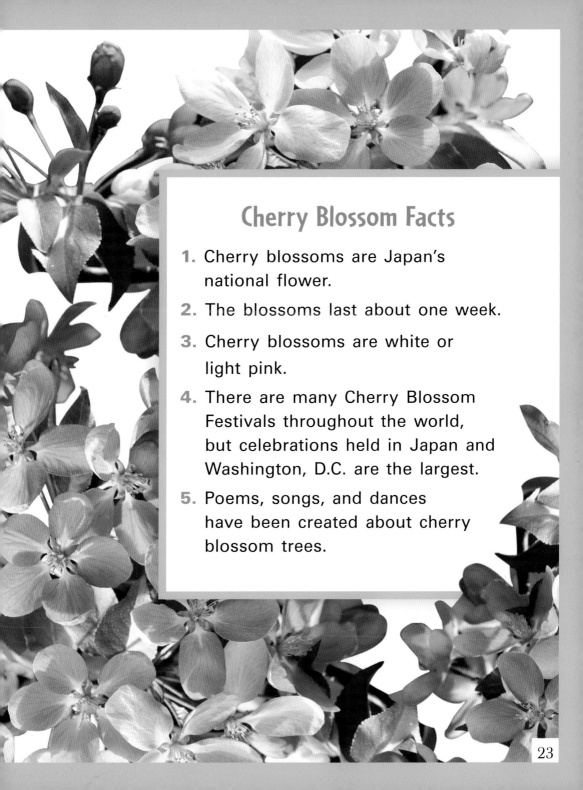

Cherry Blossom Facts

1. Cherry blossoms are Japan's national flower.

2. The blossoms last about one week.

3. Cherry blossoms are white or light pink.

4. There are many Cherry Blossom Festivals throughout the world, but celebrations held in Japan and Washington, D.C. are the largest.

5. Poems, songs, and dances have been created about cherry blossom trees.

CHAPTER 6
Sweden and Finland: Walpurgis Night

In Sweden and Finland, two countries in northern Europe, people celebrate Walpurgis Night, an important festival that honors spring's arrival.

SWEDEN

FINLAND

Helsinki

Stockholm

The event begins on the evening of April 30. Family and friends eat and sing songs as they welcome the coming season.

While the purpose of Walpurgis Night is the same in both countries, there are some differences in how Sweden and Finland celebrate it.

On April 30, people in Sweden and Finland celebrate spring with a festival called Walpurgis Night.

Walpurgis In Sweden

In Sweden Walpurgis is called *Valborg*. Part of the celebration includes lighting large bonfires at night. The bonfires began long ago when people believed that the fires kept away bad luck. Today people may spend months gathering material to burn in the fires.

Long ago the fires were made from branches that the young people of the village gathered. They were paid for doing this in eggs!

Walpurgis In Finland

Many people in Finland enjoy eating this fried treat called *tippaleipa*.

In Finland Walpurgis is called *Vappu*. Because it signals the end of winter, the day is a joyous event. Many people celebrate by wearing masks on their faces and shouting happily in the streets. Most people in Finland don't usually act that way!

May 1 is a public holiday, and schools and most offices are closed. Family and friends gather for outdoor picnics. One treat made especially for the occasion is *tippaleipa*, a sweet, fried pastry that is shaped like a bird's nest.

CHAPTER 7

Iran: Norouz

The last stop on our tour of spring festivals is Iran, formerly known as Persia. The country is in southwestern Asia and is more than 5,000 years old.

Iran's calendar was developed centuries ago and is still used today. Its new year, Norouz, falls on the first day of spring. Norouz means "new day" in Farsi, the Arabic language spoken in Iran.

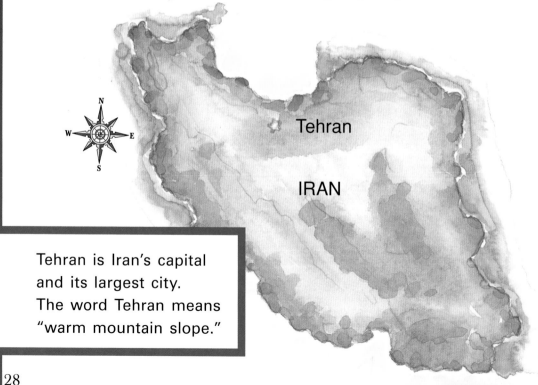

Tehran

IRAN

Tehran is Iran's capital and its largest city. The word Tehran means "warm mountain slope."

Norouz is a national festival and is celebrated by everyone in Iran. The holiday is also celebrated in Afghanistan and in countries where Iranians have moved to, such as India. It lasts for 12 days and is about joy and celebrating a new year.

No one is sure how the holiday started, but many historians think it began centuries ago in farming villages to welcome spring's arrival.

This family is feasting on traditional dishes during Norouz.

On the first day of Norouz, people often wear new clothes. They also exchange gifts and visit family and friends. Tables are filled with fruit, cakes, and other treats.

People have picnics on the thirteenth day of the festival. They also throw lentils, a green vegetable, into streams or brooks to symbolize the throwing away of bad luck.

That completes our tour of spring festivals. Celebrations are held in many other parts of the world, too. There may even be a spring festival in your community. If not, you may want to celebrate spring in your own way. Go on a picnic and enjoy the blooming flowers and the budding trees. Celebrate longer daylight hours and warmer weather. Enjoy spring!

Glossary

equator an imaginary line dividing Earth into two halves called hemispheres

harvest the gathering of crops

Northern Hemisphere the half of Earth that is north of the equator

orbit path

pollution making air and water unclean with harmful chemicals and waste products

symbolize stand for; represent

vernal equinox the first day of spring, when day and night are of equal length all over the world

Index